About the play

The People

- **Ben**
- **Tom**
- **Alice**
- **Kirsty**

They are all from a Year 9 class.

What's Happening

Ben, **Tom**, **Alice** *and* **Kirsty** *have been asked by their teacher to read part of* Macbeth *by Shakespeare.*

Ben   Right, where do we start then?

Tom   Miss said we just had to read
          a bit out loud.

Kirsty   Well, what's it about?

Tom   It's about this murderer
          called Macbeth.

Ben   Right! That's me then.

Alice   Wait a minute, wait a minute!
          How come you're Macbeth?

Ben   Because Macbeth is a murderer,
          and I'm brilliant at murderers –
          (*points a gun at* **Tom**)
          Die, slug-face! Die! Pow!

Kirsty   But what about the rest of us?

Ben   There are plenty of other parts.
          Look, there's Ross, and Duncan,
          and Angus . . .

Alice   Plenty of other men you mean.
          There are never any parts
          for women.
          He's really sexist, this
          Shakespeare.

1

Ben Well, there must be some women.
(*looking at book*)
Oh yes. Look! Three witches!
What are you moaning about?
How perfect can you get?
There are two here already made.
You won't even have to act.

Kirsty/
Alice (*together*) Oh very funny! . . .
Just watch it, you . . .

Ben It's all right. I was only joking.

Tom Miss said that in Shakespeare's
time all the women's parts
were played by men as well.

Alice Well Ben, you ought to do that.
You'd be good at that.
We all know how much you like
dressing up as a woman.

Ben What? Why you . . .

Alice (*sweetly*) It's all right.
I was only joking.

Kirsty	Did the men really play the women?
Tom	Well, that's what Miss said. She said boys played the young women, and men played the older ones. Women actors weren't allowed.
Alice	Well, that's just my point. Shakespeare was sexist. He never had women in his plays. So when we come to read it there're no parts for us!

Ben	Well, let's do the witches' bit.
	At least we'll get something read.
	Let's do their spell.
Everyone	All right then!
	All look at their books and
	read together.
	'Double, double, toil and trouble,
	Fire burn and cauldron bubble.
Ben	Eye of newt and toe of frog,
Alice	Wool of bat and tongue of dog,
Tom	Adder's fork and blind-worm's
	sting,
Kirsty	Lizard's leg and owlet's wing,
Everyone	(*all together*)
	For a charm of powerful trouble,
	Like a hell-broth boil and bubble.
Kirsty	Scale of dragon, tooth of wolf,
Tom	Witches' mummy . . .'
Ben	Wait a minute! Wait a minute!
Alice	What's the matter?
Ben	I don't understand any of this.

4

Tom	It's a spell, isn't it?
Ben	Yes, I know that, but what's a 'blind-worm's sting', or an 'owlet's wing'?
Tom	Well, I don't know. But I know what a frog is, and a bat.
Ben	Yes, but even so, they're all old-fashioned things.
Kirsty	Well, it's an old-fashioned play.
Ben	Why don't we bring it up to date?
Kirsty	What do you mean?
Ben	Well, these are all the disgusting things you put in a spell, right?
Kirsty	Right!
Ben	Well, let's put in some modern things.
Kirsty	Like what?
Ben	Well, what's the most disgusting thing in school?
Alice	French.
Ben	No, I mean something real.

Tom	I know! School dinners.
Kirsty	Oh yes, especially the custard.
Tom	Yuck! Just the smell makes me ill.
Kirsty	I know a worse smell than that – that burger bar on the way into town.
Alice	Oh yes! They fry dogs there.
	Everyone makes sick noises.
Ben	Look, that's good.
	That's the sort of thing we want.
	We ought to write it down
	so we can put it in the spell.
Tom	Good idea. Come on, Kirsty.
	You're good at writing.
	Write down what we've said.
Kirsty	All right, let me get a pen.
	What have we got then?
Alice	School dinners.
Kirsty	Oh yes . . .
	(*writing*) . . . and?
Tom	Custard.
Alice	And dogs.

Kirsty	Right. (*writing everything down*) What else?
Tom	What else smells bad around here?
Alice	Those toilets by the boys' changing rooms. They smell disgusting!
Ben	Oh yes! Get that down.
Tom	What about other things? Not just smells.
Ben	Like what?
Tom	Well, diseases and things like that.
Ben	You mean like cancer?
Alice	You can get cancer from mobile phones. It was on the news.
Tom	I don't believe that. That's just a scare story.
Ben	Well, we can still use it.
Alice	I'll tell you what I think is disgusting – the way footballers spit all the time.

Ben	That's not disgusting – that's just natural.
Alice	No it's not! Look at other games. Other people don't do it. Footballers just do it because they think it looks hard.
Kirsty	You're right, Alice. They always do it when they're getting up.
Alice	Or when they've been fouled.
Tom	My dad said David Beckham was the most disgusting thing he'd seen – when he stuck his finger in the air.
Alice	You can't blame him for that. After what those fans were shouting.
Ben	Let's put it in in any case. Have you got it, Kirsty?
Kirsty	(*writing furiously*) Yes, just about.
Ben	I'll tell you the most disgusting thing I've seen.

Alice	What's that?
Ben	That nose stud you wore
	to the school disco.
	It made your nose run all the time.
Tom	Oh yes! That was horrible.
Alice	Well, what about you?
	Remember that dirty football shirt?
	You put it behind the radiator in the
	classroom and forgot all about it.
	Two months later you pulled it
	out, and put it on!

Tom	Great! Have you got all this, Kirsty?
Kirsty	Wait a minute! Give me a chance.
	(*writing away*)
	Has anyone got anything else?
Alice	Let's hear what we've got so far.
Kirsty	All right then.
	Let's read it together.
Everyone	'Double, double, toil and trouble,
	Fire burn and cauldron bubble.'
Ben	Canteen custard
	and deep-fried dog,
Alice	Beckham's finger and smell
	from the bog.
Tom	Cancer from mobile stuck
	in your ear,
Kirsty	Spit from a striker tripped
	from the rear.
Ben	Alice's nose stud streaked
	with snot,
Alice	and Ben's football shirt
	that he forgot.

Everyone   Put in the microwave and
                simmer well.
                That's an up-to-date witch's spell.
                (*Everyone laughs*)

Ben   That's wicked.
                Our spell's the best.
                Much better than boring
                old Shakespeare.

Tom   Let's do some more.

Ben   All right then.
                (*silence*)

Alice   I can't think of any more.

Kirsty   And my hand's aching.

Tom   I suppose we do need to read
                some bits from the rest of the play.

Alice   There are still no parts for girls.

Ben   Yes there are. There's Lady
                Macbeth and Lady Macduff.

Alice   (*sarcastic*) Oh, great! Two!
                There're twenty parts,
                and two of them are women.
                And they're just wives,

| | Mrs Macbeth and Mrs Macduff –
they're not big parts. |
| **Tom** | Yes they are.
Miss said that Lady Macbeth is the
most important part in the play. |
| **Kirsty** | Why don't we just read the bits
with Macbeth and Lady Macbeth.
Then at least it would be equal. |
| **Alice** | But that's only two parts. |
| **Kirsty** | We can each take it in turns.
Then we'll all get a chance. |
| **Ben** | All right then. Everybody agreed? |

(*Everyone nods*)

| | Where shall we start? |
| **Kirsty** | Let's do the first bit
where they're together. |
| **Ben** | What's happened so far? |
| **Tom** | The king is coming to stay
with them. |

	He's called Duncan.
	Macbeth wants to kill him
	so he can be king,
	but he's too scared to do it.
Ben	How do you know that?
Tom	Miss told us.
	Some of us do listen, you know.
Ben	Right! Alice, you can be
	Lady Macbeth,
	and Tom, you can be Macbeth.
	OK then! Ready?
Tom	(*reads*)
	'My dearest love,
	Duncan comes here tonight.'
Alice	'And when goes he hence?'
Tom	'Tomorrow, as he purposes.'
Alice	'O never shall sun that morrow
	see . . .'
	(*Breaks off*)
	She's going to get him, isn't she?
	She's going to get that Duncan.

	Macbeth may be scared to,
	but she's not.
Ben	Let's carry on.
Alice	'Look like the innocent flower,
	But be the serpent under it . . .'
Ben	That's a typical woman – so
	two-faced!
	She looks like a sweet little flower,
	but is really the snake
	underneath it.
	You say Shakespeare
	doesn't know anything about
	women, but I reckon
	he's got them spot on.
Kirsty	Let's do the next bit.
	Macbeth says . . . Go on, Tom.
Tom	'We will proceed no further
	in this business.
	He hath honoured me of late,
	and I have bought
	Golden opinions from
	all sorts of people . . .'

Alice   Well, that's a typical man, that is.

Tom   What does it mean?

Alice   It means he's making excuses.

He's trying to back out.

He's saying that because

the king likes him,

and because everyone says

how good he is,

he doesn't want to do it anymore.

Kirsty   What does Lady Macbeth say?

Alice   'Was the hope drunk

Wherein you dressed yourself?

Hath it slept since?

And wakes it now,

   to look so green and pale

At what it did so freely?

From this time

Such I account thy love.'

Tom   'Prithee, peace!

I dare do all that may become a
   man.

Who dares do more is none . . .'

Alice	Oh that's typical as well, that is.
	He's all talk, that Macbeth.
	He boasts about what a man he is,
	and how he's going to do this,
	and how he's going to do that.
	But as soon as it comes to it,
	he can't do anything.
Ben	Well he is talking about murder.
	He's not just making a cup of tea!
Kirsty	What does she say next?

Alice	'I have given suck, and know
	How tender 'tis to love the babe
	that milks me.
	I would, while it was smiling,
	in my face,
	Have plucked my nipple . . .'
Ben/Tom	*snigger*
Alice	That is typical!
	You boys are so immature.
	As soon as you see the word 'nipple'
	you're trembling like jellies.
Ben	Well, it's sexy, isn't it.
Alice	No it's not!
	Listen to what she's saying.
	'. . . I would have plucked my
	(*shouts*) NIPPLE from its
	boneless gums,
	And dashed its brains out,
	had I so sworn as you
	Have done to this . . .'

See, it's horrible.

	She's saying she would murder her
	baby to get what she wanted.
Kirsty	She is pretty scary.
	I bet Macbeth's afraid of her.
Alice	He is.
	See what he says next.
Tom	'If we should fail?'
Alice	'We fail!
	But screw your courage
	to the sticking-place
	and we'll not fail . . .'

You see!
He needs a woman to give
him strength.
That's typical of a man, that is.

Tom I think it's the other way round.
When you get something
really bad, really evil,
like Macbeth here killing the king,
then there's always a woman
behind it.

	Women are much more cruel than men.
Alice	That's rubbish. Like who, for instance? Name me one woman who's more cruel than men.
Tom	Well, there's that woman, who did all those murders . . . I can't think of her name . . .
Ben	I know. It was that new maths teacher. She's the cruellest woman in the world. She'd show this Lady Macbeth a thing or two. *(Laughter)*
Kirsty	Do they actually murder Duncan?
Tom	Macbeth does. Lady Macbeth drugs the servants and takes their daggers, so they can pretend it was them.
Kirsty	Let's do that bit, then.

Ben	Let's swap round.
	Kirsty, you and me can read now.
Tom	All right then.
	It's in the middle of the night,
	and Lady Macbeth is outside
	Duncan's bedroom.
Kirsty	'Alas, I am afraid they have awaked,

    And 'tis not done . . . Hark!

    I laid their daggers ready;

    He could not miss 'em.

    Had he not resembled

    My father as he slept, I had done it.

Macbeth comes in

    My husband!'

Ben	'I have done the deed.
	Didst thou not hear a noise?'
Kirsty	'I heard the owl scream
	and the crickets cry.
	Did you not speak?'

Ben	'When?'
Kirsty	'Now.'
Ben	'As I descended?'
Kirsty	'Ay!'
Ben	'Hark!
	(*looking at his hands*)
	This is a sorry sight.'
Kirsty	'A foolish thought, to say a sorry sight.'
Ben	'There's one did laugh in his sleep, and one cried "Murder! . . ."'
Alice	One what?
Tom	One of the servants.
Ben	'. . . And they did wake each other: I stood and heard them: But they did say their prayers, and addressed them Again to sleep.'
Kirsty	'There are two lodged together.

Ben	One cried "God bless us!" and "Amen!" the other;
	As if they had seen me with these hangman's hands.
	Listening their fear, I could not say "Amen!",
	When they did say "God bless us!"
Kirsty	'Consider it not so deeply.'
Ben	'But wherefore could not I pronounce "Amen"?
	I had most need of blessing, and "Amen"
	Stuck in my throat.'
Kirsty	'These deeds must not be thought After these ways. It will make us mad.'
Ben	'Methought I heard a voice cry "Sleep no more!
	Macbeth does murder sleep . . ."'
Alice	Creepy, isn't it?
Tom	Yes – you can tell Macbeth's scared.

He's jumping at anything.

Ben   Well, wouldn't you be,
if you'd just murdered someone?

Alice   But Lady Macbeth's not.
She's much harder than him.

Kirsty   I don't know.
I think she's just putting it on.
Look at the way she says
she would have killed
Duncan herself
except he looked like her dad.
I don't think she's as hard
as she pretends.

Ben   Look, she says '. . . a little water
clears us of this deed . . .'
as though it doesn't matter –
they've got away with it.

Tom   They might have got away with it
with other people,
but not with themselves.

Kirsty   What do you mean?

Tom	Well Miss said that Lady Macbeth goes mad, and Macbeth gets haunted by the people he murders.
Ben	Does he murder some others, then?
Tom	Yes, loads.
Alice	And Lady Macbeth goes mad?
Tom	Yes! That's the famous bit.
Alice	Oh let me do that. I've always wanted to play someone mad. (*cackles*) Hee-hee-hee! . . . I'm mad . . . mad, I say! (*more cackles*) Ha-ha-ha! Hee-hee-hee . . .
Ben	Very good, Alice, but when are you going to start acting?
Alice	Don't start that again.
Tom	All right Alice, you can be Lady Macbeth. You come in from the top. You are sleepwalking.

Ben and Kirsty, you're the doctor
and the servant.
You're watching her.

Kirsty   ' . . . Lo you, here she comes.'
Ben   'You see her eyes are open.'
Kirsty   'Ay, but their sense is shut.'
Ben   'What is it she does now?
    Look how she rubs her hands . . .'
Tom   That's right. Look as though
    you're washing your hands.

Alice   '. . . Yet here's a spot . . .'

Ben   Has she got zits then?

Kirsty   Oh don't be silly.

              She's talking about spots of blood.

Alice   '. . . Out, damned spot!

                  Out, I say! . . .'

Ben   You see!

              She has got zits.

Kirsty   Oh shut up. Carry on, Alice . . .

Alice   '. . . One, two, why then,

                  tis time to do it!

              (*cackle, cackle*)

              Hell is murky!

              Fie, my lords, fie! A soldier?

              And afraid?

              Yet who would have thought

              the old man to have had so much

                  blood in him.'

Ben   'Do you mark that?'

Alice   'The thane of Fife had a wife.

              Where is she now? . . .'

Kirsty	Who's that?
Tom	One of the people Macbeth has murdered.
Alice	'. . . What will these hands never be clean?
	No more of that, my lord.
	No more of that.
	Here's the smell of blood still.
	All the perfumes of Arabia will not sweeten this little hand.
	Oh . . . oh . . . oh!'
Ben	'What a sigh is there!
	The heart is sorely charged.'
Alice	'I would not have such a heart in my bosom.'
Ben	'Well, well, well . . .'
Alice	'Pray God it be, sir.'
Ben	'This disease is beyond my practice.'
Alice	'Wash your hands.
	Put on your nightgown.
	Look not so pale.

I tell you again – Banquo's
buried!

He cannot come out of his grave.'

Ben 'Even so?'

Alice 'To bed, to bed!

There's knocking at the gate.

Come, come, come, come!

Give me your hand.

What's done cannot be undone!

To bed, to bed, to bed!'

(*The bell goes for the end
of the lesson.*)

Ben Oh there's the bell.

We've got to stop there.

And just as Alice was

coming on to me.

Well, well, well. Fancy that!

Mind you, who can blame her . . .

Alice Ben, there's just one thing I have
to say to you.

Ben What's that?

Alice In your dreams, boy! In your dreams!